790.1 FOR

Forte, Imogene.
Backyard : adventures fo
outdoor explorers.

		DATE DUE		

THE TABLETOP LEARNING SERIES

BACKYARD

Adventures for Outdoor Explorers
by Imogene Forte

Incentive Publications, Inc.
Nashville, Tennessee

For information about our audio products, write us at:
Newbridge Book Clubs, 3000 Cindel Drive, Delran, NJ 08370

Illustrated by Gayle Seaberg Harvey
Cover designed by Mary Hamilton and illustrated by Jan Cunningham
Edited by Susan Oglander and Mary C. Mahoney

Library of Congress Catalog Number 83-80959
ISBN 0-86530-091-7

THIS
BACKYARD BOOK
BELONGS TO

_____

CONTENTS

WIND, SNOW, AND WINTER SKIES

COLLECTING AND ENJOYING BACKYARD TREASURES

MYSTERY AND MAKE-BELIEVE

STAKE OUT YOUR TERRITORY

. . . First, walk all around your backyard and look at it as if you are seeing it for the first time.

. . . Next, get a big sheet of paper and some felt tip pens and make a map of the yard. Be sure to mark north, south, east, and west. Draw in the trees, paths, the picnic table, animal homes, or any other things that are important to your backyard.

. . . Count the trees and try to learn the names of ones that you do not know. Learn as much as you can about each tree—who planted it, when, and why. Find out which trees have fruit, leaves, and/or seed pods and which ones are homes for animals.

. . . Observe and keep a record for a week of all the animals that pass through the yard. Note the time of day and the spot in the yard where you saw them. Do they live there or are they just passing through? How often are they there? Are you apt to see them again? Which ones are wild animals and which ones are pets?

. . . Make a list of all the plants that you know the names of. Think about who planted the ones that are cultivated and why. Try to find out how the weeds got where they are.

. . . Is the temperature hot, cold, or in-between? Read the thermometer at the same time every day and keep a temperature record for one week. Find out what time the sun rises and sets.

. . . If you don't have a backyard of your own, don't despair—adopt a backyard (with the owner's permission, of course). It might be a vacant lot, space in a nearby park, or someone else's yard. Remember, there is a lot going on in your backyard. The purpose of this little book is to help you to enjoy it more.

Imogene Forte

A LITTLE DETECTIVE WORK

WHO IS WATCHING WHOM?

If you really want to get acquainted with the animals in your backyard, you are going to have to develop some patience and devote some quiet time to it.

First, you should place either a nice flat rock or a plastic cushion in a central location where you can go and sit for a while on most days. You will want to make sure that the spot you choose will not be too sunny or too shady, and that it is comfortably located (not too close to a noisy street or to weeds and shrubs or tall grass that might be filled with creepy-crawlies).

You should go to your observation post at the same time every day, seat yourself, and wait quietly for the action to start. The slightest, sudden noises or movements will frighten the animals and cause them to scurry out of sight. If you sit perfectly still, however, these backyard residents will go about their business of scratching for worms, spinning webs, burying nuts, or carrying on their natural activities.

Take a book or some drawing paper and crayons with you and wait for the show to start. Soon the animals will take your presence for granted and they may be as interested in you as you are in them. After a few days, it will be hard to tell who is watching whom!

BACKYARDS ARE FOR SMELLING

Early in the morning while the dew is still on the grass is the best time to take a backyard-smelling walk.

Pick a nice, warm, spring morning for your walk. Move around slowly and quietly and enjoy the stillness of the morning. Stop in a lot of different spots and sniff the good fresh air. Notice how the smells differ in some spots. Try to decide which smells are coming from natural growing things and which smells are caused by pollution.

Look around for some good-smelling plants. Bend over to smell the low flowers and shrubs, jump high to smell leaves on the trees, or stretch out flat on your tummy to bury your nose in sweet-smelling grass.

Some especially interesting smells that you may be lucky enough to find are: just-mown grass; roses in full bloom; lilies of the valley; lilacs and hyacinths; peppermint and spearmint leaves crushed between your fingers; sage, lemon balm, and thyme; eucalyptus; honeysuckle, and ripe strawberries on the vine.

You might want to capture some of these wonderful smells for your house. If so, make the potpourri on the following page.

Some plants, such as marigolds and chives, have a distinctive smell that is not especially pleasing to most people. Others, like the skunk cabbage, are downright unpleasant. Then there are many plants that have no smell of their own to speak of.

Just sniff around awhile and give your nose some exercise. You will be surprised how much better acquainted you can become with the sights and sounds as well as the smells of your own backyard.

15

SPICY POTPOURRI

Use cinnamon sticks, cloves, dried flower petals, and allspice to make a spicy potpourri as a gift or for yourself. Mix the cinnamon, cloves, and flower petals in a mason jar. Sprinkle with allspice and leave for a week.

Then put a handful in a net bag and tie with a ribbon or put the potpourri in pretty bottles. Either is a nice way to hold on to some of nature's lovely smells.

CATCHING DEW DROPS IN A JAR

Did you ever wonder exactly how much dew falls in your backyard?
Here is a simple experiment that will help you find out.

You will need to collect: a shovel or hoe, a piece of plastic (a piece of a garbage bag will be fine), four heavy rocks, a jar with a tight fitting lid, and a lot of patience.

Here is what you do . . .

Dig a shallow hole in the ground. Before dark, place the plastic piece in the hole. Push the sides of the plastic around until there is a little well in the center. Put a rock on each corner to hold the plastic in place. The next morning, lift the plastic out carefully and pour the dew that has collected into the jar. If you do this every day for a week, you may be surprised at the amount of dew you have collected.

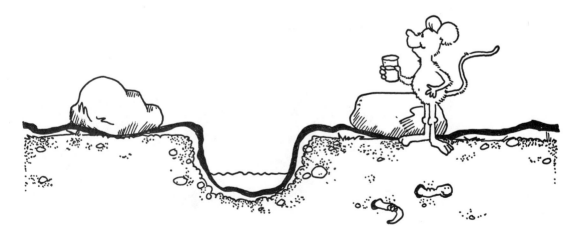

INSPECT A NEST

Try to find a last year's bird's nest on the ground. If you see one left in a shrub or tree, make sure it is an old one no longer in use by watching for a few days to see that there is no "bird traffic" to and from it.

Take the nest apart carefully to see what materials the builder used. You will most likely find some things peculiar to your own backyard.

PROVIDE A DO-IT-YOURSELF KIT FOR A NEW NESTER

Fill a net bag, the kind onions or fruit come in, with some of the following things:
- small pieces of brightly colored yarn or string
- small, lightweight twigs
- straw
- stalks of dried grass
- old rubber bands (cut apart)

Tie the filled bag to a low tree branch that will be easy for the birds to get to and carry things away from.

If you're a good detective, you may discover your scraps in a new nester's nest.

INVITE YOUR FINE-FEATHERED

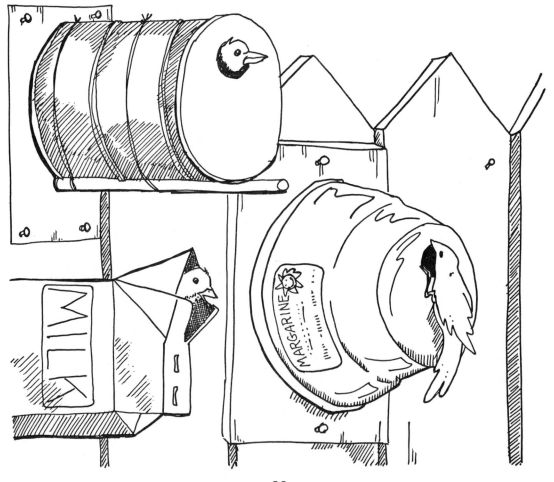

GET TO KNOW A TREE

Pick your tree. Tie a ribbon or a string around the trunk of the tree to tell everyone that this is the tree that *you* are getting to know.

Walk around the tree several times. Then stand back and look carefully at the tree. Begin by looking at the roots, then the trunk, letting your eyes move slowly from the bottom of the trunk all the way to the top. Look at the branches, where they begin, and how they grow.

Put your arms around the tree to feel how big the trunk is. Then run your hands up and down and around on the tree trunk to see how the bark feels.

Take a big sniff or two to smell the tree.

Sit down under your tree for a while. Think about . . . the tree's scientific name; how old you think the tree is; if the tree was planted by someone, or if it grew "on its own" because of a seed carried by the wind or a bird or dropped from another tree. How does the tree help or harm other plants or animals?

Some things you can do as you and your tree are getting acquainted: ☐ Draw or paint a picture of the tree on the day that you select it. Save the picture. ☐ Draw or paint a new picture during the year to show how the tree changes with the seasons. Date the pictures to show when the buds and leaves form, how they grow, and when and how they fall. If you choose

an evergreen tree, you can watch the pods or cones grow and fall, and show these changes in your pictures. ☐ Listen to and watch the wind blow through the branches of the tree. ☐ Find out if your tree has leaves, flowers, seed pods, and/or fruit. ☐ Try to discover what animals live in or on or visit your tree. If you watch carefully and patiently, you might see many types of birds, squirrels, and insects. ☐ Collect and press some leaves at different times during the year. Save the leaves and glue them on a sheet of paper

(one leaf from each season). It will be interesting to see how this poster shows the changes in color, size, and texture of the tree's leaves.

HEAR, HERE

Ask a friend to join you for a backyard "Hear, Here" party. Provide paper, pencils, an alarm clock, and a snack for two. Find a nice shady spot and sit a few feet from each other. Set your clock's alarm for five minutes. Close your eyes and listen to the sounds. You may be surprised at how many different sounds you hear when your ears are turned "on," and your eyes and lips are turned "off."

When the alarm goes off, open your eyes and quickly list all the sounds you heard. Exchange papers and read each other's list. Without discussing the lists, set the alarm for five minutes and close your eyes again. This time, listen *especially* for any sounds that were on the other person's list that you did not hear, and of course there will be some new sounds that were not on either list.

When the clock signals the end of five minutes this time, open your eyes and your snack sacks and enjoy discussing the sounds you have just heard and their sources.

24

GET ACQUAINTED WITH A BUG

Capture one of those creepy-crawlies or winged beauties. Remember not to go for poisonous insects or those that might sting you. Avoid spiders too.

Make one of these cages to hold your captive just long enough to let the two of you become better acquainted. Then open the cage wide and the two of you can go about your own business.

BEWARE OF THESE!

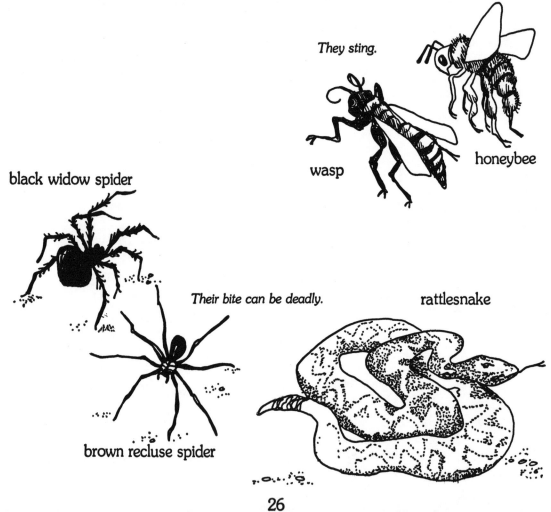

They sting.

wasp

honeybee

black widow spider

Their bite can be deadly.

rattlesnake

brown recluse spider

26

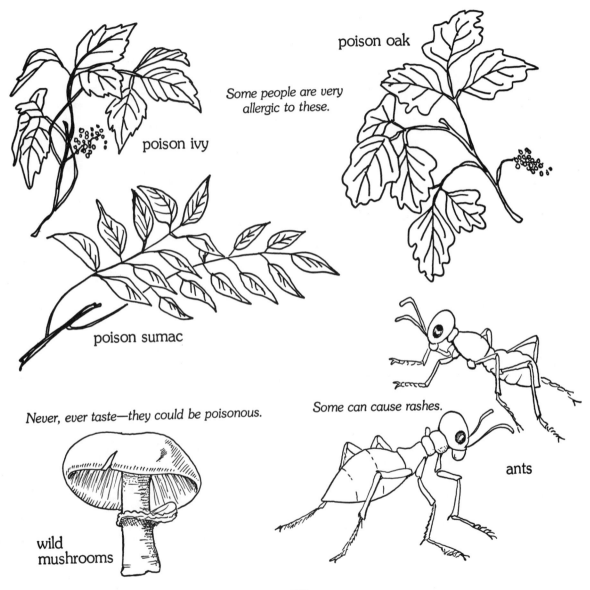

poison oak

Some people are very allergic to these.

poison ivy

poison sumac

Some can cause rashes.

ants

Never, ever taste—they could be poisonous.

wild mushrooms

BE A BACKYARD SPECIALIST

You can become a specialist in your own backyard by finding answers to these questions. Your friends will be amazed at how smart you are when you ask questions like these that only you have the answers for. Actually, even you may be impressed by how much you know. Besides, you will have had fun learning a lot of marvelous and mysterious things you never even thought about before now.

Read these questions through carefully. By the time you have finished all the activities and projects, you should have answers for most of the questions. Check the ones left unanswered and plan your strategy. To complete work toward becoming a backyard specialist, you may need to make a trip to the library, ask a grown-up for some help, or just do a little more detective work.

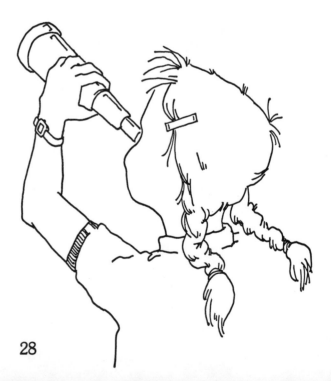

???QUESTIONS???

☐ How many different kinds of trees are in your backyard? Name the kinds. ☐ How can you tell how old a tree is? ☐ How many animals actually live in your backyard? ☐ How many different kinds of animal homes are located in your backyard (nests, burrows, cocoons)? ☐ How do the animals that live in your backyard protect themselves from enemies (bee/stinger, hen/beak, kitten/claws, turtle/shell)? ☐ How many animals that live in your backyard make musical sounds (birds, frogs, crickets, owls)? ☐ What was your backyard before it became your backyard (vacant lot, wooded area, part of a big estate)? ☐ What kind of clouds tell us rain is on the way? ☐ What causes a rainbow? ☐ At what temperature do you need a sweater to feel comfortable in your backyard? ☐ How do the weeds and flowers that grow in your backyard differ? ☐ How many of the plants provide food for birds? For people? For squirrels and/or rabbits? ☐ What would happen to the flowers and weeds if there were no bees?

SUNNY SKIES
and
SUMMER DAYS

BACKYARD HIDEAWAYS FOR HOT SUMMER DAYS

Drape an old sheet over a picnic table. Leave an opening for the door. Cut some windows in the back and sides to let you see out.

Cut a door and windows in a big packing box (the kind refrigerators or washing machines come in). Decorate it to suit your fancy—you could make a bus, theatre, castle, log cabin, space station, or something only you can imagine.

Set up a big beach umbrella and spread your blanket under its shade.

Use boards and cushions to make a tree house if you have a tree that is safe and if you check with the grown-ups first. Tree houses don't have to be fancy to be fun.

Find a good spot behind or inside a clump of bushes or vines and "hollow out" your own spot.

Make a circle of short stakes and put a tall stake in the center of the circle. Attach twine or string from each short stake to the tall stake. Plant pole beans at the bottom of each short stake. Help wind them along

the string as they grow and when they reach the tall stake, you will have a special hideaway. (You will need some patience for this one. It takes from 45 to 60 days for the bean vines to grow enough to make a hideaway.

33

WATER, WATER EVERYWHERE AND NOT A DROP TO DRINK

On a hot summer day, find one or two friends who don't mind being wet, jump into your bathing suits, and get set for a friendly water war.

Draw a big circle on the grass with chalk and appoint the first caller. (You can take turns doing this.) Each person will need a big bucket of water, some sponges, and two or three plastic spray bottles (the kind window cleaner and liquid soap come in).

Everybody fills bottles and sponges with water from the buckets and takes a place on the circle. When the caller begins the game, players start to chase each other around the circle, squirting water from the bottles and throwing sponges at each other. When a player is forced outside the circle, he/she is out of the game. The person left in the circle is the winner of the water war.

Sit in the sun to dry off before you go back to refill your buckets for the next round.

SUMMER DAY PICTURE

A few materials and a few extra minutes will give you a nice reminder of this summer. Keep it and take it out on a snowy winter day. It will give you a warm, happy feeling.

You need: grasses, dried flowers, weeds, fern fronds, and other natural materials from the yard; cotton fiber; picture frame with glass; blue, red, and yellow dry tempera paint; paper baking cups or a muffin tin, and waxed paper, newspapers, and heavy books (for drying).

Here's what to do:

Press the natural materials if they need it. Put the plants or flowers between waxed paper and then between piles of newspapers with heavy books on the top. Smooth out the cotton so it will fit the picture frame. Put each color of dry tempera paint in a separate baking cup. Add a little water. Dab some paint on the cotton in the frame and begin to make the background for your picture. Blend the colors to create a summer feeling. You will be working with three colors, so mix them to get as many shades as possible. (You might want to leave some area white for variety.) When the background is finished and dry, arrange your natural materials on the picture. Place the glass and frame over the scene and secure it. If you work very carefully, you will not need glue because the glass will hold your arrangement in place.

STAGE A BACKYARD CLEANUP

Even the neatest-looking and best-kept backyard in the whole world almost always has some clutter and trash that needs cleaning up. You might be surprised! How much trash do you think you can find in your backyard? Celebrate Earth Day on April 22 (or the first Saturday after Earth Day) by cleaning up your own backyard.

You will need a big shopping bag for trash, a pair of good strong gloves, and a cardboard box for any materials that can be recycled.

First, walk all around the yard to spot items that need to be picked up. Look for pieces of plastic containers, paper, bottles, aluminum cans, cardboard, and other litter that might be hiding in the grass or shrubs.

Then put your gloves on, grab your bag, and get started. Pick up all the litter you can find. If you find any bottles and cans, put them in the box to be recycled. Carry the other stuff in the bag to your back door and ask the people in your house to come out and admire your efforts before you deposit your "litter" cargo in the garbage cans.

The first EARTH DAY celebration was held April 22, 1970.

FOLLOW THE POPCORN TRAIL

Use popcorn to mark a secret trail for a friend to follow to find a surprise. The surprise could be two big bags of popcorn—one for the friend and one for you. Some of the popcorn might disappear due to "other" friends along the way!

CELEBRATE IN YOUR BACKYARD!

Invite your family to a cookout. First, think about your family, what they like to do, and what they like to eat. Next, look around your backyard and think about when and how you would enjoy a special cookout. Think about the perfect cookout for your family. Then plan the cookout. When will it be, where in the backyard, how will you cook, what will your menu be? Invite the family and get to work.

You will need to make plans for: a menu (including shopping, costs, and preparation time); things to use, tablecloth, and tableware (paper and plastic or from your kitchen); help in preparation and cooking if you need it (be sure to ask a grown-up for help with the grill or bonfire—this is a must!); CLEANUP—a big trash can or bag for throwaways.

WHIZ BE

RAKE IN THE GOODIES

If you try this cookout one time, it's a sure bet you'll adopt it and use it over and over.

You'll need these things: bonfire, rake, hot dogs, buns, condiments, and marshmallows.

Here's what to do . . .

Ask a grown-up to help you sterilize the rake. Hold it over the coals for a minute or two to clean it. After the rake cools, place one hot dog on the prongs of the rake for each person. Hold the rake over the coals to cook the hot dogs. When the hot dogs are cooked, remove them and place the opened buns on the rake, using the rake as a grill. Serve the grilled hot dogs and toasted buns with your favorite condiments. For dessert, place marshmallows on the prongs and toast them over the coals until they are cooked the way you like them.

BRRR—THIS IS ONE COLD LUNCH

"Cool off" on the hottest Saturday of the summer with an ice-cold lunch. Start by making sunny honey tea. Fill a quart jar with water. Add two or three tea bags and put the lid on the jar. Set the jar in a sunny spot—indoors or outdoors—for about three hours. When the tea looks dark, remove the tea bags. Stir in some honey and serve over ice with a slice of lemon. This should serve four or five thirsty friends.

Serve: cold-cut roll-ups (bologna, ham, or roast beef with a little mustard or cream cheese rolled up inside and stuck with a toothpick), a pickle, celery curls and carrot sticks, a cold potato, sunny honey tea, and a popsicle.

Wrap the food in foil or plastic kitchen wrap and pack in tins such as those coffee or shortening come in. You will need one for each person so you will want to start your container roundup before you issue the invitations. If you can't find enough containers, clay flowerpots or small sand buckets will work, but not as well as the containers with tops that keep them airtight.

Fill in all the spaces around the food with ice cubes and close the containers until lunch time. It will be fun to see your friends "shiver and shake" as they eat.

WIND, SNOW,
and
WINTER SKIES

THANK HEAVEN FOR THE STARS

In ancient times, when shepherds spent the nights under the stars watching their sheep, they imagined they could see kings, queens, maidens, and monsters in the stars. Look up in the sky and use your own imagination. What do you see?

Stars have helped guide sailors, travelers, hunters, and campers. You too, can use the stars to find which way is north by finding the North Star. Follow these directions. Locate the Big Dipper—four stars make up the bowl, three the handle (actually the second star in the handle is really two stars, but you must have good eyesight to see them). The two stars farthest from the handle will guide you to the North Star. Imagine a line drawn through them and extend it about five times the distance between the two stars. The North Star is at the end of the handle of the Little Dipper. If you move your eyes to the horizon directly under the North Star, you will be facing due north.

On a winter's night, wrap a blanket around you, make some hot chocolate, and go outside to gaze at the winter stars. If you start from the Big Dipper and look south, you will see Orion. Two bright stars make up his

44

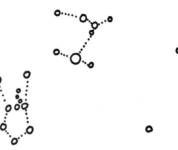

shoulders, three small stars form his head and two more form his legs. Three close stars are his belt and three more make up his sword. Look closely to see what other constellations you can see. If you look to the left of Orion's belt, you will see Sirius. Next to our own sun, it is the brightest star in the sky.

MAPLE SNOW CREAM

Make a snow treat that will melt in your mouth!

Scoop some clean snow into a large bowl. Pour ¾ cup cream over the snow. Slowly add 1 cup real maple syrup, stirring gently as you pour. Quickly divide the snow cream into as many bowls as there are people to serve.

PURE
MAPLE
SYRUP

THE WIND WILL BE MUSIC TO YOUR EARS

To make a nifty wind chime you will need to use: a medium-size clay flowerpot, adhesive tape (this holds better than masking tape), brightly colored macramé cord or yarn, different-size nails, scissors, and aluminum pie tins.

Cut the pie tins into different shapes (hearts, diamonds, strips, half-moons). Punch a hole near the top of each shape. String the shapes onto pieces of the cord or yarn (several on each cord). Tie nails onto some other pieces of cord. Tape the ends of the cord pieces to the rim of the flowerpot. Cut several long pieces of cord the same length. Twist the pieces together and tie a knot on one end to make a hanging cord. Pull the end without the knot through the hole in the bottom of the flowerpot and tie a strong knot to hold it in place. Tie your wind chime to a low branch of a tree and let it tell you which way the wind is blowing.

NATURE'S FORECASTERS—
THE CLOUDS

Have you ever looked up at the clouds and seen an animal, face, or other familiar shape? Clouds form in all sorts of patterns and shapes, and besides looking like imaginary figures to us, they also tell us a lot about our weather. Pick a day to spend some time in your backyard observing the clouds.

Here are some of the things clouds can tell about weather on the way:

If the clouds are wispy and featherlike, they are *cirrus* clouds and usually indicate clear weather.

High clouds that give a complete overcast to the sky are called *cirrostratus* clouds and generally mean rain is on the way.

Fine weather cumulus clouds are fluffy, small clouds. If they are spread out in a clear sky the weather is nice; if they look like they are in rows before noon, the weather will probably turn bad.

Thunder, lightning, and sometimes hail come from clouds called *cumulo-nimbus,* which are low in the sky and continuously change shape.

cirrus

fine weather cumulus

cirrostratus

cumulonimbus

49

SOME OTHER THINGS THAT DANCE ON THE WIND

Here's how to make a paper airplane and a pinwheel.

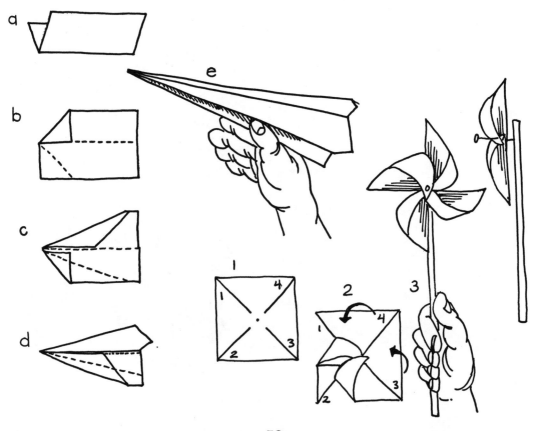

BACKTRACK A FRIEND

Ask a friend to join you for a backtrack game in the snow. The game works like this:

You and the friend stand side by side in the untracked snow. Look around the backyard and plan together a walk that will make a circle around the entire backyard. Then shake hands and turn back to back. You go one way around the yard, and your friend goes the other way, taking care to make good strong footprints in the snow as you go. You should pass each other along the way as you continue around the circle until you are both back where you started.

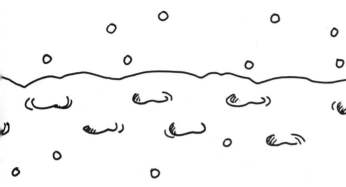

Then the fun begins. You again shake hands and turn back to back. This time you each go around the circle in the other person's tracks, but walking backward instead of forward. The object of the game is to see who can step out of the tracks the fewest times as you go around the circle.

Regardless of the outcome, the two of you will have some jolly fun following the circle around the third time to determine who the winner really is!

FOLLOW THE TRACKS

Go outside early in the morning when your backyard is blanketed with new-fallen snow. Walk slowly and carefully around the yard looking for animal tracks. See if you can find any of these.

squirrel

skunk

cat

rat

raccoon

woodchuck

P.S. If it never snows where you live, you can look for backyard tracks the day after rain has left the earth damp.

mouse

PREHISTORIC SNOW CREATURE

Amaze your friends and neighbors with a snow creation beyond belief. Create a Snowasaurus, a Brontosnowrus, or name your own prehistoric snow creature.

Add the finishing touch by cutting out two large feet from heavy cardboard. Tie the cardboard feet around your own feet and walk around the creature to make "tracks."

COLLECTING and ENJOYING BACKYARD TREASURES

THINK BEFORE YOU TAKE

True nature lovers learn to collect and enjoy backyard treasures by look-ing, listening, smelling, touching, tasting, and by thinking and remembering.

A flower just unfolding or a butterfly on the wing can become a more beautiful memory than a pressed posy or a dead insect. Greedy collectors sometimes plow through backyards and woodlands snatching and grabbing everything in sight, without thought. It's good to begin to collect things that you really want or need and to be sure that what you take does not disturb the balance of nature.

Collect only things that are pleasing to you and that you think you will treasure for a long time, or that you want to give to someone else to enjoy. Before you decide to make things, think about why you are making them and what you will do with the finished product. And you don't always have to *make* something out of the things you collect. Some of them are more beautiful in their natural state than they are painted or glued together. A plain bouquet of colored leaves will bring a bit of autumn splendor to a teacher's desk, and your friends might prefer a jar of shiny stones to use for a Rocky Guessing Game more than a painted rock paperweight.

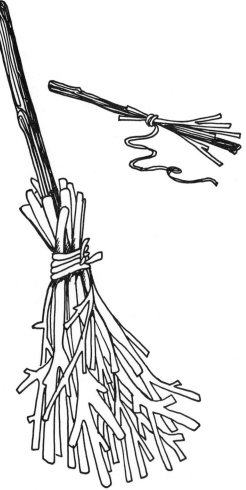

BROOM OF TWIGS

Here's some help to sweep up the fallen leaves.

To make your own broom, you will need: a straight tree branch about 1½ inches thick and 2 to 3 feet long, twine or string, and several straight twigs.

Tie the twine tightly around the thick branch approximately 8 inches from one end. Arrange about a half dozen of the straight twigs around the branch and bind them together with the twine. Continue adding more twigs until you have a nice-size broom, tying each one into place. Bind them all together very firmly. You can use weeds if you can't find enough twigs.

JEWELRY RACK

Make a holder for all those rings and things.

To make a gift for someone else or a treat for yourself, start with these things: a sturdy tree branch or piece of driftwood, soap and water, scrub brush, old cloth, gold or silver paint, small paintbrush, and liquid wax.

Look for an unusually shaped tree branch or piece of driftwood. Try to find one with several prongs of different sizes and shapes. Scrub the wood with soap and water, using the brush to get into the crannies and holes. Be sure to remove all sand and dirt. Dry the wood thoroughly with the cloth. Streak the wood with silver or gold paint to add interest. Follow the natural grooves or curves in the wood if possible. Add a coat of liquid wax to the wood to preserve the finish.

SEED SENSE

When the blossoms of the flowering plants, weeds, and trees have been replaced by seed pods, take some jelly jars to the backyard and collect seeds. Be sure to label the jars and keep each set of seeds in its own jar. (Don't take all the seeds from any one plant—always leave some to drop to the ground and start new plants.)

Here are some things to do with the seeds:

Make seed pictures on construction paper, strips of old, weathered board or tree bark.

Save some of the seeds to plant next year. (Some plants are annuals and have to be replanted every year, some are biennials and must be replanted every two years, and others are perennials and come back each year.)

Plant some in small pots, put them on your windowsill, and watch them grow. (Giant oaks *do* grow from tiny acorns.)

Print the names of the plants on envelopes, draw pictures to show how the plants look, decorate the envelopes, and give as gifts.

Combine all the seeds in a bucket or pie tin and use as a bouquet for the birds on a cold, cold day next winter.

Use white glue and smaller seeds to create designs on sheets of plain white paper to make elegant stationery or greeting cards.

Most important of all, look carefully at each plant and its seeds. Compare the size, color, and feel of different seeds. Make a note of where each plant grows and check there next year to see if the plant reseeded itself and new plants are growing near the old.

CAPTURE A LEAF FOR YOUR WALL

You will need the following: leaves; aluminum pie tin; cooking oil; plaster of Paris; water; paper clip; green, gold, or red poster paint, and clear shellac or liquid wax.

Here's what to do:

Grease the aluminum pie tin with cooking oil. Arrange the leaf or leaves in the bottom of the pie tin. Mix the plaster of Paris and water according to the directions on the package (you can count on using half as much water as plaster). When the plaster of Paris begins to harden, push the paper clip into the plaque to make a hanger. When the plaster has hardened completely, cut the pie tin away and peel it off. Take the leaves off the plaque. Paint the leaf impressions the color of your choice. If you want to make your plaque more permanent, cover it with a coat of clear shellac or liquid wax.

ROCK GARDEN CREATION

Gather together the following things: shoe box top, dirt, rocks and pebbles, small mirror, moss, and twigs.

Then follow these steps:

Choose a shoe box top for your rock garden. Turn it upside down and cover the inside of the lid with a thin layer of dirt. Use a small mirror from an old compact (or any small mirror you can find) to make a reflecting pool. Place this strategically in the box. Place different types of moss at the pool's edge. This will form a lush bank and give the pool an attractive border.

Stick twigs between the clumps of moss.

Add a large rock near the water's edge.

Make a curved path with small pebbles leading to the pool. Place other twigs, moss, and rocks in your shoe box top to finish your enchanted rock garden.

MYSTERY and MAKE-BELIEVE

JUST IMAGINE

You are a king or queen for a day . . .
Make a crown for yourself and wear it all day.

Sweet clover, daisies, feathers and leaves, can make magic crowns quick as you please.

SET A TRAP FOR A UNICORN

Legend says that a unicorn is a mythical, horselike animal with a single horn in the middle of its forehead.

Check out a book from your library that tells about unicorns or other legendary beasts. Try to find one with some good illustrations. Find a nice shady spot in your backyard and sit down to read and enjoy the book. After a while, think about the kind of trap you might build to catch a unicorn or other marvelous exotic creature if one just happened to cross your backyard. You might build a big circle out of stones with a magic opening just big enough to get in but not out.

Hollow out a trick opening in the shrubbery. Use sticks and boards with a leafy camouflage or place a mirror on the ground to attract and hold the creature so you can tie it to your favorite tree, or use your imagination to create your trap.

Check your trap in a day or two to see what you have captured. You won't be disappointed if there is no unicorn, will you? After all, a nice person like you would certainly have set the unicorn free again. Besides, you probably don't know one other person in the world who has built a unicorn trap in the backyard, so that makes you a very special person.

LET YOUR FINGERS BECOME . . .

All you need is bright sunlight, a plain wall, a little skill, and a lot of imagination. Keep your eyes on the shadow rather than on your hand, and you can create a variety of animals. You can make them fly, wiggle, and walk too! To add a spark of mystery and make-believe, try . . .

- a dinosaur
- a unicorn
- an enchanted swan
- a winged horse
- monsters in several sizes

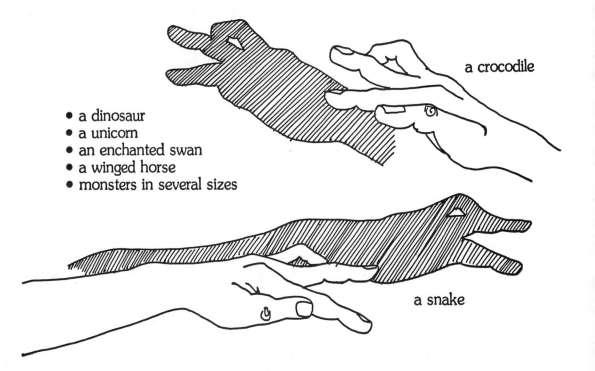

a crocodile

a snake

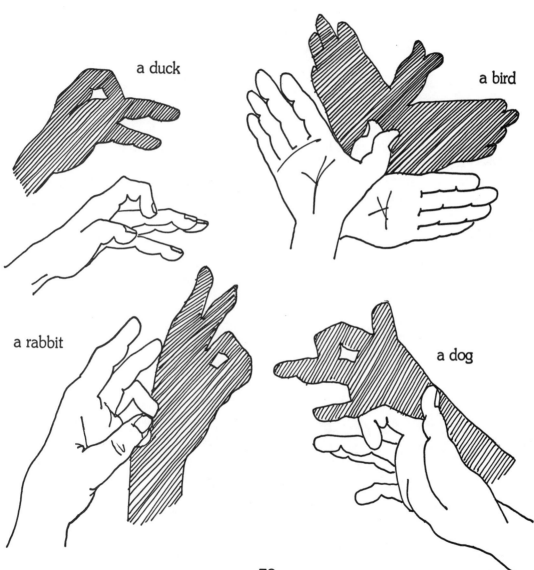

a duck

a bird

a rabbit

a dog

73

BACKYARD
FAIRY FOLK

Are you sure there are no leprechauns or other fairy folk in your backyard? When was the last time you looked?

Early some morning, when the sun is just coming up and the backyard is still sparkling with dew, explore the territory by looking under sticks and stones, between the leaves of trees and stems of plants, into the buds and flowers and holes in the ground—*everywhere* for signs of the fairy folk.

How many of these can you find?

- ☐ a spider web
- ☐ a shamrock
- ☐ mushrooms or toadstools
- ☐ acorn cups for nectar
- ☐ hummingbird feathers
- ☐ pink clover
- ☐ fern
- ☐ pieces of tree bark
- ☐ a clear, polished magic stone
- ☐ periwinkle shells
- ☐ a frog that just might turn into a prince
- ☐ splendid colored leaves
- ☐ forked branches
- ☐ fairy wings
- ☐ star moss
- ☐ lilies of the valley
- ☐ beans—like the ones Jack planted for his beanstalk

Gather as many of these as you can into a pile and sit down to make up a story about the friendly fairy who left them behind. Tell your story to someone who believes as you do (just a little bit) in backyard fairy folk.

75

LIGHT UP YOUR NIGHT

Most night creatures use their senses of sound and smell to operate in the nighttime sky. But fireflies blink the lights on their abdomen for a visual signal to other fireflies. Chemical compounds interact with oxygen to make cold light that the insects flash generally when they are forming pairs or are disturbed. Light up your night sometime soon with some fireflies.

In the early evening, capture some in a jar (be sure to punch holes in the lid for air). Look closely at the jar and watch the lights flicker—then let the fireflies go.

THE SUGAR PLUM TREE

For a special treat that serves as a centerpiece as well, make a sugar plum tree. Your guests will love ending their backyard feast by "picking" dessert right off its branches.

Look all around your backyard until you find an interesting tree branch with lots of little twigs and prongs. Stand the branch up in a flowerpot or big bucket. Fill the pot or bucket with small stones and/or gravel to hold the branch up straight. Use yarn or ribbon to tie hard candies, lollipops, peppermint sticks, marshmallows, gumdrops, packages of nuts and raisins, and cookies to the branches of the sugar plum tree. (Use plastic kitchen wrap to wrap any of the sweets that do not come already wrapped.)

Select a combination of goodies that you think will make a pretty tree and that you think will be good to eat. If your budget allows, you may want to add ice cream bars to complete the treat.

A SNOW QUEEN'S CASTLE

The winter months are a perfect time to make ice creations in your backyard. And if it stays really cold, your ice creations will last for several days. All you need are odds and ends from the kitchen and some water. You can use margarine containers, ice cube trays, cupcake pans, cookie molds, funnels, basters, plastic meat trays, plastic soda straws, plastic toy packaging and other plastic, rubber, or metal containers from the household. Be sure that you don't use glass containers because they will expand and break. It is a good idea to use molds that are larger at the top or straight-sided so the ice can be removed easily. Be sure you wear gloves to handle the metal molds or the metal will stick to your skin.

Take your molds and containers outside on a freezing day and fill them with water. You might want to add a few drops of food coloring to the water

to make your ice creations colorful. Leave them until the water freezes solid.

When you are ready to start building your ice castle, check the temperature of the air and make sure it is at or below freezing. Dip the molds into a pail of warm water for a few minutes until the ice shape slides out easily. You may use a spray bottle of water to freeze-weld the ice pieces together. If there happens to be snow on the ground, this will help in holding some of the initial walls together.

You are ready to create your ice castle! You will find that the margarine containers make domes; ice trays make bricks; cupcake pans make thick discs; cookie molds make decorations for towers; funnels (plug the small hole with modeling clay) make spires; basters make tall spires; plastic meat trays make patterned designs for roofs and walls; soda straws make bridges or ways to connect towers; and clear toy packaging will make interesting shapes if you use your imagination.

You'll end up with an ice castle to suit a snow queen!